TAXATION

PAYING FOR GOVERNMENT

Charles Hirsch

A Blackbirch Graphics Book

RSVP

RAINTREE STECK-VAUGHN
P U B L I S H E R S

Austin, Texas

A Blackbirch Graphics Book

Printed in Mexico.

1 2 3 4 5 6 7 8 9 0   RRD   97 96 95 94 93 92

Library of Congress Cataloging-in-Publication Data

Hirsch, Charles, 1946–
        Taxation: paying for government / Charles Hirsch.
        (Good citizenship library)
        Includes bibliographical references and index.
        Summary: Examines the history of how and why governments collect money and discusses the Internal Revenue Service and taxation in the United States.
            ISBN 0-8114-7356-2   ISBN 0-8114-5584-X (softcover)
        1. Taxation—History—Juvenile literature. 2. Taxation—United States—History—Juvenile literature. [1. Taxation. 2. United States. 3. Internal Revenue Service.] I. Title. II. Series.
HJ2250.H57   1992
336.2'00973—dc20   92-5198
                                                              CIP
                                                              AC

Acknowledgments and Photo Credits

Cover, p.7: ©Blackbirch Graphics, Inc.; p. 4: ©Riha/Gamma-Liaison; p. 10: Bettmann Archive; p. 14: North Wind Picture Archives; pp. 16, 17, 32: Library of Congress Collection; p. 18: ©Mary Lauzon; pp. 21, 26, 28, 40: ©Bruce Glassman; p. 24: ©Steve Winter/Gamma-Liaison; p. 30: ©Yvonne Hemsey/Gamma-Liaison; p. 35: ©Stuart Rabinowitz; p. 36: ©Stephanie FitzGerald; p. 38: AP/Wide World Photos; p. 42: ©Cynthia Johnson/Gamma-Liaison; p. 44: ©Don Jones/Gamma-Liaison.

Photo research by Grace How

Contents

Taxes and the

World We Live In

Jackie is 11 years old. Her mother is a police officer. Her father is the principal of Martha Washington High School. Jackie likes gymnastics and Nintendo games. Her favorite television program is "Mr. Wizard's World."

Jackie's mornings are usually pretty routine. "But not this morning," she told her friends later that day. Today, she really had to wake up early. Too early. Gymnastics practice started at 7:00 A.M. and she had to leave the house by 6:30. The sleepy-eyed Jackie went into the bathroom to splash some water on her face, but there was no hot water. In fact, there was no water at all!

Opposite:
Sanitation workers, firefighters, and police are just a few public servants who are paid with tax money. Here, two police officers walk their beat through a Chinese neighborhood in Los Angeles.

5

"No hot water," she yelled down the hall.

Soon Jackie's mother was at her daughter's side. She was carrying a pot of warm water that she had heated in the microwave.

"Here," she said, "this is your morning shower." Then she smiled as she poured the warm water into the sink for her daughter to use to wash up.

Jackie wasn't the only one without water that morning. The water in the entire neighborhood was turned off. The pipes were so old that the city water department had decided to replace them. And this was the morning they began the work. The work would last for only a few days, but it was going to cost hundreds of thousands of dollars. Those dollars would come from a fund created by city taxes.

What Are Taxes?

Taxes are payments to a government. Taxes can be paid to a city, a state, or the federal government. The payment can be a "percentage," a part, of what something may cost when you buy it. For example, when Jackie bought her last Nintendo game, she paid five percent of the cost of it in "sales tax." (That equals five cents for every dollar that something costs.)

Taxes can also be a percentage of what a person earns in wages or what a business earns in profits. This is an "income tax." Jackie's mother and father pay "income taxes" on their salaries.

Opposite:
A cost added to your purchase at the cash register is the sales tax on that item. Video games, CDs, and magazines are just a few items that carry a sales tax for the buyer in most states.

And taxes can also be a percentage of what something is worth. Each year Jackie's parents pay a percentage of what their house is worth. They pay this in the form of a "property tax" to their local city government.

Their property taxes pay for the improvements on the water pipes. They also pay for Jackie's mother's salary as a police officer. They partly pay Jackie's father's salary as school principal. The other part of his salary is paid from "state income taxes."

Jackie's older brother, Scott, is an air force pilot. Taxes pay for the plane he flies and the uniform he wears. Tax money even pays for the food he eats at his base. The tax money to pay for Scott's work in the military comes from the "federal income tax" collected by the Internal Revenue Service.

What Are Taxes For?

As you see, taxes pay for many things. They pay for Jackie's gymnastics equipment at school. In fact, tax money paid for the school itself.

Taxes pay for many of the things that people need in order to live better lives. The government provides education that prepares people to be productive citizens. The United States armed forces provide national defense. Firefighters and the police provide protection at home so that we can feel safe.

All of this is done at great expense. Local, state, and federal governments must raise the money to pay for these goods and services through taxes.

Taxes and Your World

This book introduces you to the issues and problems of taxation in the United States. Taxation refers to the system of collecting taxes. The issues and problems of taxation are many. Right now, we will look only at those that most affect your life.

Taxation is almost as old as government itself. Thousands of years before Jackie's parents paid taxes and benefited from them, families in ancient Greece and Rome did likewise.

Those people in ancient times probably complained about paying too much in taxes, just as people do today. However, if we did not pay taxes, our government would come to a halt. Schools would close. Roads would fall apart. We would have no police officers or firefighters to protect us. Can you imagine what life would be like?

Someday you will vote to elect our leaders. You can gain an understanding of how taxes can build a better nation by learning about how taxation works. Then you can make the wise decisions all Americans must make in electing their leaders.

You will want to vote for leaders who will govern fairly. You will want to vote for leaders who will see that the money you pay in taxes will be well spent. You will want to vote for the leaders who will provide a safe, productive nation for you and your family. And you will want to vote for leaders who best represent your beliefs.

The History

of Taxation

Throughout history every known government has had some kind of tax system. Taxes are the price citizens must pay for government services and goods.

In ancient times taxes were paid by the citizens of Athens, Greece, to build their beautiful temples. And the people of ancient Rome paid many taxes to support their army, construct enormous stone bridges, aqueducts (water systems), and great roadways. Their system of bridges and roads and their great army made Rome the most powerful nation in the ancient world. And it was Spanish tax money that paid for Christopher Columbus's voyage to the new world in 1492.

Opposite:
Most great civilizations of the past were paid for with taxes. Egypt, Greece, and Rome all relied on taxes to build great cities and to supply powerful armies.

11

Today, too, tax money supports our armies and pays for buildings, roads, and bridges. Tax money also paid for voyages on which we have made great discoveries. Without tax money we could not send women, men, and machines to explore outer space.

A History of Greed, Corruption, and Terror

Most people accept the expenses of government. Unfortunately, the history of taxation has also been a long story of greed and corruption. A look at this history clearly shows that taxes can build a nation or destroy it.

The earliest records of a tax system date back to about 3500 B.C. Scientists have discovered writings on clay tablets in what is now Iraq. These clay tablets describe in part how the governments of ancient civilizations operated. They also tell about the system of taxation that was used. Even then, greedy government officials discovered how to control the citizens of a country. They made the people they were supposed to govern into pawns of the state through excessive taxes. A saying on one of these tablets reads, "You can have a lord, you can have a king, but the man to fear is a tax collector." Since citizens were required to pay taxes, tax collectors were often accompanied by armed soldiers who saw to it that taxes were collected, even if by force.

The people of ancient Egypt were forced to pay taxes on everything they owned. They had to pay taxes on earnings from their jobs. But they also had to pay taxes on their property, cattle, crops, pets, and even home gardens. Farmers were given grain and told where and when to plant it. A portion of each year's harvest, which could be grains, honey, or even cooking oil, was collected as tax.

The government hired scribes who were similar to accountants. They kept the financial records of the people. They determined how much tax people paid, and they also collected those taxes. The scribes, however, were never required to pay any taxes. As might be expected, many of these scribes became dishonest. They added revenue from taxes to their own personal wealth.

The people of ancient Egypt resented this. However, those who were unwilling or unable to pay their taxes could be beaten or sold into slavery. Some pharaohs (ancient kings of Egypt) spared their people such punishment. They did not want to overburden their people with too many taxes. They feared that if they did, the people might possibly revolt.

Tutankhamen was one such pharaoh. He made an attempt to stop the corruption of dishonest scribes by cutting off their noses before sending them to a remote part of Arabia. We know that he actually did this. Historians have found records that describe a colony of people with deformed faces that lived in Arabia. King Tut's practice might not have stopped all corruption, but it certainly helped.

Tutankhamen was a pharaoh in ancient Egypt who tried to stop corruption and unfair tax practices in his society.

A Story of the Wish to Be Free

The ancient Greeks are an example of a people who succeeded in creating a fair system of taxes. Very few taxes were demanded. Those that were necessary were not large. And they were paid voluntarily. The Greeks were eager to give what they could to make their nation great. They had tremendous pride in their country. Many huge and beautiful buildings were erected by wealthy citizens who were seeking honor. Even the poor, who were unable to give money, gave freely of their time and their labor.

In its early stages, Rome operated much like Greece had. In their free time, people volunteered their labor. This meant that fewer taxes were required. Gradually, however, the Roman government demanded more and more of its people. Finally, the Roman citizens revolted.

One of the bloodiest tax revolts occurred in Rome in 88 B.C. The Roman government was robbing its citizens not only of their belongings, but also of their self-worth. With nothing to call their own, citizens lost

One of the bloodiest tax revolts in history occurred in Rome in 88 B.C. Citizens rose up against the government that was making slaves out of the people by over-taxing them.

their feeling of pride and their satisfaction in daily living. It was while an important leader of the government, a man named Sulla, was away fighting a foreign war, that the people rose in revolt. In total, many thousands of Roman tax collectors and businessmen were killed in the uprising.

The Jewish people have carried heavier taxes for longer periods of time than any other nation. In the Book of Exodus, the Bible speaks of the unusually harsh taxation of the Jews when the Israelites lived under Egyptian rule in the 1200s B.C. After that time, the Jews were enslaved by other foreign governments—Assyrian, Babylonian, Persian, Roman, and German. These rulers demanded extremely high and unjust taxes from the Jews.

Did We Learn the Lessons of History?

Spain was once the most powerful nation on earth. Indeed, its rule during the 16th century stretched around the globe. Its eventual ruin, however, can be traced in part to its system of taxation. As was customary, Spain demanded high taxes from its new subjects and sought to make slaves of the conquered people by taking away all that they had. Spain's greed caused the taxpayers throughout its territories—the Americas, Africa, Caribbean islands, and the Philippines—to revolt. These revolts led to Spain's eventual downfall.

England, too, suffered the harsh consequences of trying to overtax its new subjects. The original

In the year 1765, a cry was heard throughout the 13 colonies: "Taxation without representation is tyranny." The American colonists resented the tight control England kept on them through the enforcement of tax laws. The colonists argued that their interests should be represented in England's Parliament if that was where taxes were decided. They had already rebelled against some British taxes—those on molasses, newspapers, and imported goods, among others. Now England was trying to sneak in an additional tax—on the tea imported into all British colonies. Tensions between the colonists and the British government grew quickly.

In Boston, on the night of December 16, 1773, a large group of colonists disguised themselves as Indians and boarded three British ships that were laden with tea. Before the night was over, they had dumped 342 crates of tea into Boston Harbor. This event, known as the Boston Tea Party, sent a spark through the colonies and rallied support for a full-scale revolution against England.

13 colonies that became the United States rebelled against their mother country, England, because of unjust taxation. The Revolutionary War (1775 to 1783) successfully freed American colonists from English rule and English taxation.

Decade after decade, as our country grew, however, so did the need for increased taxes. From time to time, Americans found it necessary to rebel when taxes became too heavy. In the United States during the 1990s protests against high taxes are becoming more common. Voters in several states have voted to stop extravagant government spending. They have, in fact, voted to stop higher taxes. Today, voting is our form of tax revolt.

The Revolutionary War was the result of England overtaxing its colonies in America. George Washington (on horseback) led American troops to victory in the Revolution.

CHAPTER 3

Kinds of Taxes

The United States was still young. It was only 13 years old when the great American statesman Benjamin Franklin wrote:

> OUR CONSTITUTION IS IN ACTUAL OPERATION; EVERYTHING APPEARS TO PROMISE THAT IT WILL LAST; BUT IN THIS WORLD NOTHING IS CERTAIN BUT DEATH AND TAXES.

Congress had levied its first tax on its citizens in 1789. It did so in the form of a "tariff." A tariff is a tax on goods that are brought into a country from other countries. Since that time, the citizens of the United States have been expected to pay many other kinds of taxes.

There is probably no other country in the world that has resisted paying taxes more than the United

Opposite: Gasoline carries a tax of its own. Usually, the money collected from gasoline taxes helps to pay for the construction and maintenance of our various transportation systems.

States. The first colonists used their muskets and cannons against England to protest excessive taxation. Certainly, when the United States won its independence, its citizens had no intention of taxing themselves in the way England had done to them for so many years.

What Goes out Must Come In

The good intentions of the Founders of our country had to be put aside when the Congress realized it had no money to run the government. How would new roads be built? How would the mail be delivered? Who was going to pay the president of the United States? More important, who was going to pay Congress itself for its services? Members certainly were not willing to work for nothing. Taxes were the only answer. And taxes are still the only answer.

Our country requires schools and up-to-date textbooks to educate its young people. As our people live longer lives, we need to build more senior-citizen housing that will be safe and comfortable. We need to maintain the roads that crisscross our nation. We need an increasingly larger police force to battle violent crime. And once we put criminals in jails, we need tax money to run the jails and prisons. We need to pay the salaries of our park rangers. Without them, such places as the Statue of Liberty, Yellowstone National Park, or the Florida Everglades could not exist.

Opposite:
Different kinds of state and city taxes help to pay for schools and other public needs.

As these and the other needs of government have increased, so has the need for higher taxes. During its first years, our nation could rely on the voluntary contributions of its productive citizens. But that could not go on forever. Until the Civil War broke out in 1861, the government was chiefly financed by the tariff on imports. It was also financed by excise taxes (taxes on goods made or sold within the country) on tobacco, whiskey, carriages, sugar, and other products. Finally, it was supported by taxes on land, buildings, and slaves.

A Taxing Situation

Most Americans will agree with Benjamin Franklin about "death and taxes." Ask your parents or your teacher. They may not know what the weather will be like tomorrow, or what kind of car you will be driving in ten years. But they will agree on the certainty of paying taxes. The kinds of taxes most people think about first are income taxes. Although this is the largest source of money that the government takes in, there are other kinds of taxes.

Note that the chart on page 23 shows only two items that aren't a kind of tax: "borrowing" and "other." For each dollar the government spends on goods and services, 12 cents is borrowed from various sources. This money comes from U.S. banks and others around the world. The money called "other" comes from such things as fines and money that other countries repay the United States.

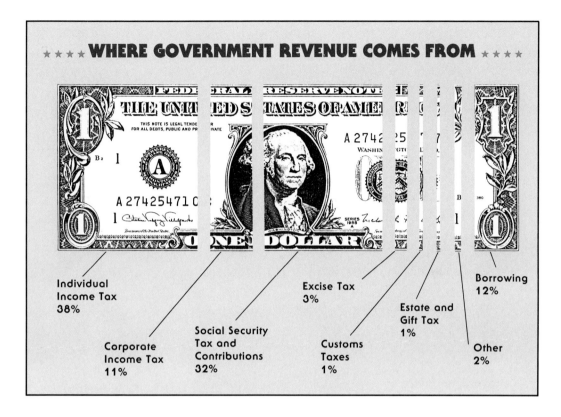

★ ★ ★ ★ **WHERE GOVERNMENT REVENUE COMES FROM** ★ ★ ★ ★

Individual
Income Tax
38%

Corporate
Income Tax
11%

Social Security
Tax and
Contributions
32%

Excise Tax
3%

Customs
Taxes
1%

Estate and
Gift Tax
1%

Borrowing
12%

Other
2%

   The remaining 86 cents that the government
spends for goods and services comes from the
following taxes.

   Individual Income Tax. This kind of tax is
often referred to as a "personal income tax." Most
individuals or families in the United States must pay
a personal income tax. What people pay depends on
how much money they earn from their jobs. It can
also be money earned from investments in the stock
market, interest earned on a savings account, or
money won from a lottery or made from selling
goods. The rent a landlord collects is also subject to
individual income tax.

23

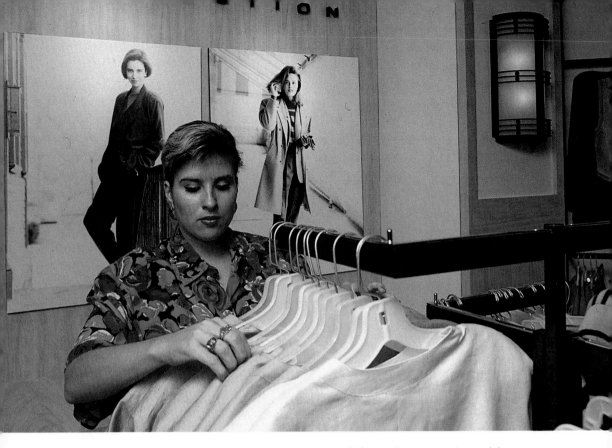

Corporations pay the U.S. government taxes on their yearly income. That means the prices marked on the goods you buy reflect the corporate taxes paid by the company that produces the item.

Corporate Income Tax. Corporations like McDonald's or The Gap pay taxes, too. They pay the government a certain amount of money on what they earn each year. That means a certain amount of what you pay for a hamburger at McDonald's or for a sweatshirt at The Gap goes to the U.S. government in the form of taxes.

A very complicated formula is used to decide how much must be paid. The taxes either you, your family, McDonald's, or any other business must pay are based on "taxable income." The taxable income is the amount used to figure what is owed to the government. It is not simply all the income of a person or business. It is the income after subtracting the "deductions," "adjustments," and "exemptions" from the total, or "gross income." Deductions are expenses such as hospital or doctor bills and interest payments made on loans. Adjustments may be portions of income that aren't taxed, such as all or part of social security payments. An exemption is an exact dollar amount that is not taxed for each dependent child of a taxpayer.

Social Security Tax. When a worker receives his or her paycheck, a certain amount of the salary is withheld. Some is withheld for federal income tax. And some is withheld for social security tax. Social security money is used by the government to help older people who are retired, people who are disabled, and people whose source of support stopped paying or died. The social security tax also pays for "Medicare." Medicare is a government program that pays for the health care of older people. In most cases, the recipients of this care paid for it in taxes earlier in their lives.

Unemployment and Workers' Compensation Tax. Money is also withheld from wages to pay for unemployment and workers' compensation taxes. These taxes go to joint state and federal funds. One of these funds pays money to people who have lost their jobs. Another fund makes payments to people who have been injured at work. The tax covers these kinds of payments, along with Social Security and medical payments.

Excise Tax. Excise taxes are placed on certain goods made in the United States. The goods taxed

Excise taxes are taxes placed on luxuries, such as perfume, alcohol, and tobacco products. These taxes tend to be higher than other kinds of taxes placed on goods.

are usually ones considered "luxuries," or not necessary. Perfume, alcohol, and tobacco are considered luxuries. Sometimes an excise tax helps pay for services for those who purchase an item. The excise on gasoline, for example, helps pay for roads. An excise may have to be paid for certain privileges. The stamp that is put on a hunting license, for example, is paid for by this kind of excise. Certain types of services, such as public utilities (gas and electric companies), also pay excise taxes. So do businesses that process natural resources, like lumber and natural gas.

Customs Tax. The very first tax that Congress placed on U.S. citizens was a customs tax, or "tariff." It is a tax placed on goods imported from another country.

Estate, Inheritance, and Gift Taxes. When someone dies, that person can leave property and money to a friend or relative. Taxes may have to be paid both from the property that was left (estate tax) and by the one who receives it (inheritance tax). Or people can also choose to give away some of their property before they die. If they do, the property is called a gift. The one who gives a gift may have to pay a tax on it (the one who receives it doesn't). Whether estate, inheritance, or gift taxes have to be paid depends on the total value of the property. It also depends on how much any one person gets, and how the people who get it are related to the one who leaves or gives it. These taxes may have to be paid to the federal government or to a state, or to both.

Still More Taxes

In addition to what the federal government collects, state and city or local governments collect still more taxes. Different states may collect the following kinds of taxes.

State and Local Income Tax. The tax money paid by individuals and corporations is a major source of income for state and local governments. These taxes are computed and collected in the same way as the federal government collects taxes. The individuals or corporations, however, do not pay nearly as much to a state or local government as they do to the federal government.

Sales Tax. When you buy a notebook marked 89 cents, why do you end up paying as much as 94 cents for it? This is no riddle. The extra five cents is the "sales tax."

Many state and local governments place a sales tax on certain goods and services. It is compiled as a percentage of the sale or the cost of the service. For example, the five-cent sales tax on the notebook is six percent of its price. Sales taxes differ from state to state. Each individual state determines its own sales tax rate. And each state also decides which goods are not subject to the sales tax (often food and clothing).

Property Tax. If you are reading this book at school, chances are the desk you are sitting at was paid for from money raised by a "property tax." The people who own buildings, land, and other property in your community pay property taxes on what they own. This tax represents a percentage of what the local government estimates the property is worth.

Many cities, towns, school districts, and counties have a property tax. The money collected in property taxes often helps to run the local government. This money is also used to help pay for road repairs and important services, like snowplowing or trash removal along roads. It pays the salaries of police officers and firefighters. And, yes, property taxes probably paid to build and maintain the school you go to every day.

Opposite:
Property taxes placed on land, buildings, cars, and other property help to pay for community services in your city or town.

4

The Internal

Revenue Service

The Internal Revenue Service is the federal agency (service) that collects tax money (revenue). It collects this money from citizens and businesses that are within (internal) the area governed by the United States. Most people refer to the Internal Revenue Service by its initials, IRS.

Although the IRS was not formed until 1862, the need to collect taxes existed from the beginning of our country. Today people may complain about the amount they pay in taxes. Some people may even refuse to pay taxes. Others provide the government with false information about what they owe. If they are caught, these people can go to jail. Tax fraud (giving the wrong information about income) is a serious crime in America.

Opposite:
The IRS collects and processes tax forms submitted to the U.S. government each year by every citizen and business in the entire country.

Alexander
Hamilton, the
first secretary of
the U.S. Treasury,
asked Congress
for the power
to increase
government
tax collection.

In 1789, the United States "levied," or placed, its first tax, which was the tariff. Two years later, it levied its second tax.

The secretary of the treasury, Alexander Hamilton, asked for power to collect more taxes. This was necessary because the government needed to raise more funds. The Tax Act of March 3, 1791, was passed by Congress in order to give Hamilton that power. The act allowed taxes to be placed on imported goods and tobacco products. It also stated that public and private makers of whiskey and other liquors had to pay taxes on their products. The act gave the Treasury Department the power to collect all these revenues. The Treasury Department still holds this power today.

Even in 1791, our government knew that any tax would be unpopular. However, it thought a tax on tobacco and whiskey would anger people the least. Both tobacco and whiskey were thought of as luxuries. They both were things that were not essential. Therefore, a tax on them created little hardship. But soon more taxes were added. These included taxes on carriages, slaves, sugar, grain refining, houses, and land.

The Civil War and the Founding of the IRS

The kinds of taxes and the way they were collected did not change much from Hamilton's time until the Civil War. When Abraham Lincoln was elected in 1861, he found that the federal debt was climbing. That meant the government was spending more money than it took in from taxes. Then the Civil War broke out. To pay for it, Congress was forced to take action. It passed the Revenue Act of July 1, 1862. This act called for taxes on all manufactured goods, and it created the tax system that is still used in our country today.

The Revenue Act was also responsible for the creation of the office of the commissioner of Internal Revenue in the Treasury Department. The commissioner was to be in charge of the Bureau of Internal Revenue. This office would handle the collection of taxes. In the beginning, the bureau was quite small. It consisted of the commissioner, George S. Boutwell of Massachusetts, and three clerks. By January of 1863, the bureau had grown to almost 4,000 employees. It remained at this level for the next 50 years. In 1920, the bureau actively employed 15,800 persons—and by 1970 the IRS numbered 70,000 workers. Today, 120,000 people work for the Internal Revenue Service—to check the nearly trillion dollars in taxes collected each year.

How the IRS Works Today

In 1952, a committee of Congress looked at the Bureau of Internal Revenue to see if it needed to be changed. Their work, along with the studies of former President Herbert Hoover, contributed to the restructuring of the bureau.

First, the name changed from the Bureau of Internal Revenue to the Internal Revenue Service (IRS). Second, each of the district branches was reorganized into the following divisions:

The Administration Division. This division manages the day-to-day work of the IRS, such as staff management, interoffice communications, and policy decisions.

The Audit Division. This division decides which returns must be examined for auditing. An "audit" is a check on what people report on their tax returns. The Audit Division studies all tax returns except for alcohol, tobacco, and firearms taxes, which are administered elsewhere. It also

Tax Returns Processed—1989

Individual income tax	110,252,723
Corporate income tax	4,208,980
Estate tax	54,700
Gift tax	121,294
Employment organizations	28,930,432
Exempt organizations	490,129
Employee plans	1,632,975
Excise taxes	948,726
Other taxes	52,927,407
Total Tax Returns	**199,567,366**

provides assistance to taxpayers who ask for help. And finally, it helps in the investigation of people and businesses that cheat on their taxes.

The Collection Division. This division consists of two branches. First, there is the office branch. The office branch collects unpaid accounts and past-due returns through letters, telephone contacts, or by office appointments with the public.

Tax forms supplied by the IRS are used to show the government how much tax is owed by American taxpayers each year.

and given tax-exempt status.

• Social welfare organizations and charities

• Nondiscriminating nonprofit clubs formed for pleasure, recreation, or other activities

• Employee retirement fund groups

• Credit unions

• Corporations organized by farmers' groups

• Churches, temples, and synagogues

• Religious groups and organizations

• Community organizations established for religious, charitable, scientific, educational, literary, or public-safety testing purposes

Not everyone pays taxes. Congress has decided that certain groups or organizations do not have to pay taxes. These groups are called "tax-exempt" groups. Tax-exempt groups work in areas of public and private social service. They do not make a profit. Some of the special tax-exempt groups are:

• Special corporations that are created by the U.S. government

• Hospital service organizations (except laundries)

• Chambers of commerce

• Real estate boards

• Pension plan trusts

• Organizations for members of the armed forces

• Political groups set up for purposes of the selection, appointment, nomination, and election of public officials.

The second branch is the field branch. It seizes property of people who owe taxes. It also assists workers in the district offices around the country.

The Intelligence Division. This division employs special agents to investigate violations of tax laws. America has strict laws about violating proper tax procedures.

How do these divisions of the IRS keep track of so many people and so many businesses?

Forms, Forms, and More Forms

Each person filing income taxes receives a form that must be completed and mailed in to the IRS. On this form, each person must list how much money he or she earned from work, stocks, interest on bank accounts, and other sources. Taxpayers can deduct amounts for certain expenses, and determine how much they owe the government. Many people ask their employers to pay a certain amount of each paycheck to the government in taxes. That way, most of the tax is already paid when tax time comes. Sometimes a person determines that the government owes her or him money. That happens if more money than necessary was withheld by employers from paychecks during the past year.

There are many different types of forms. The most common forms are the 1040, the 1040A, and the 1040EZ. The 1040 form lets taxpayers itemize. That means that taxpayers can deduct, or subtract, from their income the money they spent on certain

★★★★★★ WHAT IS AN AUDIT? ★★★★★★

When a mistake is found in a person's or corporation's filed tax report, the IRS may audit, or review, the tax return. It may study a taxpayer's records for one or more years. The IRS then decides if the wrong information was reported accidentally or on purpose. If it finds that wrong information was filed on purpose, the person or corporation is subject to a fine.

Often, a 25-percent penalty, or one-quarter of the taxes owed, is placed on guilty taxpayers. According to the IRS Department of Information in Philadelphia, 8 out of every 100 people who filed income taxes during 1989 were audited. This was a total of 883,140 people.

One famous audit was that of Willie Nelson, the country singer. He was investigated by the IRS in 1984. The IRS found that he underpaid his taxes for the six years before that. He claimed that his firm (the people who took care of his money interests) gave wrong information. And that, he says, is why he paid too little tax.

The IRS says that Nelson owes $16.7 million in back taxes, penalties, and interest. Nelson is suing his accounting firm. He tried to get the IRS to wait until the lawsuit was settled, but it wouldn't. As a result, Nelson has had to sell off almost all of his personal belongings. That includes his ranch, gold and platinum records, posters, and musical instruments.

But individual taxpayers aren't the greatest source of tax frauds. The Internal Revenue Service estimates that major corporations illegally avoid paying some $20 billion in taxes each year.

Willie Nelson

things. They might be items they bought for their job. Or they could be medical expenses—money they paid to doctors or for medicine. Money you pay to church or temple or charitable organizations can also be deducted. Even the amount of money taxpayers pay to have their taxes computed can be an item to deduct.

The 1040EZ form is a shortened form of the 1040A. It is the simplest tax form. To use this form, a person must be single, have an income of less than $50,000, and not claim any "dependents" (a spouse, children, or others). The person using the 1040EZ form must have an income consisting only of wages, tips, and interest of $400 or less. The person cannot be age 65 or over, or blind. That's because senior citizens and blind people have special deductions that require another form.

Understanding which form to use might take some time! That is why, in most cases, the IRS mails the forms right to your house in January. Forms can also be found at most banks, IRS offices, or post offices in your neighborhood.

These forms must be completed and sent in to the IRS each year by midnight, April 15. If money is owed to the government, payment should accompany the forms. After the forms have been completed and sent in, the IRS processes them. If the IRS agrees that a taxpayer has already paid too much tax from past paychecks, it sends a refund check to the taxpayer.

Tax Dollars:

Paying for Government

If this book is a school or public library book, it was paid for by tax money. The park that you play in and the community pool you use are also paid for by taxes. The list of goods and services that taxes pay for goes on and on.

The taxes collected from your parents, teachers, and other taxpayers make it possible for the government to continue to operate. Tax dollars help ensure America's growth. Tax dollars also help ensure that Americans continue to be cared for.

Raising Taxes—What Can Be Done?

The problems of paying for the government of the United States are the subject of much debate. Do

Opposite:
Lawmakers spend most of their time discussing how federal tax money should be spent and how America should pay for the programs lawmakers create. These lawmakers meet in the Capitol building, in Washington, D.C.

we pay too much or too little taxes? There are no easy answers to questions about taxes. These questions have been asked ever since taxes were created.

Political leaders from the president on down have strong opinions on the subject. Newspaper editorials continually discuss the question. No two tax experts agree on the answer.

If income taxes are raised, that means that more money is taken out of a person's paycheck. Hardly anyone wants that to happen. Yet today many of the heads of America's largest corporations are saying that we must raise taxes to reduce our national debt and improve our country's services. They are also saying that we must cut government spending.

Current Issues

America's social and political problems are wide ranging. Here we will look at three specific areas that may affect you. These areas are education, transportation, and the military.

Education. You have already read about the ways property taxes and funding from the federal government make your education possible. From grade school through college, taxes pay teacher salaries, fund scholarships, and finance student loans. Tax money purchases the textbooks and visual aids you use in your classroom. It also pays for constructing and remodeling school buildings.

Without this money, the kind of education you receive would not be possible. However, critics of

Taxes are almost always the central issue in any political campaign. In 1988, George Bush made his promise of "no new taxes" the focus of his campaign.

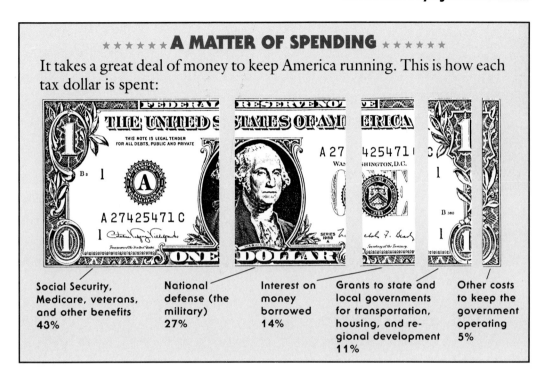

★ ★ ★ ★ ★ **A MATTER OF SPENDING** ★ ★ ★ ★ ★

It takes a great deal of money to keep America running. This is how each tax dollar is spent:

| Social Security, Medicare, veterans, and other benefits 43% | National defense (the military) 27% | Interest on money borrowed 14% | Grants to state and local governments for transportation, housing, and regional development 11% | Other costs to keep the government operating 5% |

our educational system say that even today the quality of our schooling is already falling behind that of other nations.

Transportation. Imagine if our roads were to fall apart. The products and services we use would not be as easily available. Some experts believe this is already happening. They say that without more federal spending our highways and roads will be in serious trouble. Some say that many of America's bridges are in danger of collapsing soon. Engineers remind us that when a bridge, tunnel, or road collapses, it causes long delays in getting products to their markets. And this causes millions of dollars in lost revenue, harming America's businesses and the whole economy.

43

More tax money is spent on the U.S. military than on any other sector of our government.

The military. The billions of dollars that we spend on the Stealth bomber, our battleships, our army and navy is called "defense spending." This is our largest output of tax dollars.

Many people say we can cut our defense spending. They say this because governments that only a few years ago were our enemies are now our friends. They point to such countries as Poland, Hungary, and Czechoslovakia. These countries were once Communist governments. Now they are democracies. Even the republics that formed the Soviet Union are now struggling to use elements of democracy. Many people hope we can now shift our spending from the military to local projects that require more tax dollars.

No Simple Solutions

The United States government has already decided to cut military spending. As these cuts take effect, the companies that make the fighter-jets, submarines, and missiles lose business.

If the U.S. government spends five percent less per year on defense over five years, 1.3 million jobs will be lost. Everyone from the people who design high-tech helicopters to the people who work in cafeterias on military bases will suffer. This would only add to the jobless problem. Some of these jobless people could even become homeless.

The U.S. government can, however, shift some of the billions in defense spending to other areas.

The government can shift defense spending to the areas of education and transportation. People who lost jobs in military work might then work on re-building our highways and schools.

Shifting government spending is not the only way to help pay for government without raising income taxes. Americans pay one of the lowest gasoline taxes in the world. If we increase that tax by four cents a year, in five years we would have $18 billion more in taxes.

Since 1951, alcohol and cigarette taxes have increased only slightly. Some tax experts suggest doubling the cigarette tax. They want to increase the beer tax by 4 times and the wine tax by 18 times, creating about $7.5 billion more tax dollars.

These are only some ways in which the govern-ment can raise more tax dollars without raising income taxes. There are many who agree with these ideas. And there are those who say we are already paying too much in taxes. They say what's needed is not more taxes, but less spending.

One thing is certain: We will never be tax-free. The government will always need money to oper-ate. We will always have social problems that require government spending. The issues and questions surrounding taxation will continue as long as we have people and governments on this planet. The words of Benjamin Franklin will echo through history: "In this world nothing is certain but death and taxes."

Glossary

adjustments Portions of income that aren't taxed, such as all or part of social security payments.

audit Formal checking on what people report on their tax returns.

debt Amount owed to someone else.

deductions Expenses such as hospital or doctor bills, and interest payments made on loans.

excise Tax mostly on luxury items, such as perfume, alcohol, and tobacco, and on certain privileges and services.

exemptions Amount not taxed for each dependent child of a taxpayer.

fraud Giving the wrong information about income.

interest Fee paid for the use of money.

itemize To deduct certain business, charitable, or medical expenses from one's taxes.

levy An imposing and collecting of a tax.

revenue A government's income from taxes.

revolt To rebel against the government.

tariff Tax on goods that are brought in from another country.

tax Payment of a percentage of income for the support of a government.

tyranny Cruel and unjust use of power.

For Further Reading

Patterson, Charles. *Thomas Jefferson*. New York: Franklin Watts, 1990.

Sapinsley, Barbara. *Taxes*. New York: Franklin Watts, 1986.

Schleifer, Jay. *The Declaration of Independence*. Brookfield: The Millbrook Press, 1992.

Schlesinger, Arthur M., Jr., ed. *The Internal Revenue Service*. Broomall: Chelsea House, 1990.

Spiselman, David. *A Teenager's Guide to Money, Banking, and Finance*. New York: Julian Messner, 1987.

Stein, R.C. *The Boston Tea Party*. Chicago: Childrens Press, 1989.

Index